# "NICE TO MEET YOU"

# "NICE TO MEET YOU"

by

Katherine Traphagen

All characters, places, events, and situations
in this story are purely fictional.  Any
resemblance to reality is coincidental.

ISBN 1-58500-631-9

1st Books-rev. 5/25/00

## About the Book

Eleven year old Connor refuses to accept his parents' impending divorce. Instead, he boldly takes matters into his own hands by setting up an on-line dating service. To insure that all of their dates will be miserable, he matches up his parents with people causing grief in his own life. If he can discourage them from dating other people, then just maybe, they will give each other another chance.

(Written in screenplay format.)

# OPENING SHOT

The opening is an aerial sweep showing a typical middle class suburban community. It includes houses, mini-malls with restaurants, a park with a baseball diamond, and a school. Accompanying music should be pleasant.

**FADE IN:**


**INT. GUIDANCE OFFICE - DAY - ON CONNOR AND JEAN**

**CONNOR is fidgeting uncomfortably. He is an awkward eleven year old. His tousled auburn hair spills over crooked glasses.**

> CONNOR
>
> But you're wrong!

**JEAN, is a guidance counselor in her mid-thirties. She is wearing a prim suit and large plastic rimmed glasses. Her attitude is smug and superior.**

> JEAN
>
> The point I'm trying to get across to you is that it's not what happens on the outside that makes your life. It's how **you** handle the events, because **you** can determine the effect they will have on **you**. Do you understand?

**Connor sulks silently.**

> JEAN
>
> Your parents' divorce doesn't have to be a negative thing in your life. I'm trying to help you understand that.

**Connor gives her a look.**

> JEAN
>
> You are just making it hard for yourself.

> CONNOR
>
> How do you know? They're not your parents!

**JEAN**

No, they're not my parents, but that doesn't mean I don't understand the situation.

**CONNOR**

But you're not in it, so what do you know about what's best? They're **my** parents. I know they still love each other, and I know they belong together. This divorce is all wrong!

**JEAN**

But they've decided to divorce. It's up to them isn't it? It's really not your decision to make.

**CONNOR**

But they should stay together. I just know if they made more time to be together and try again it would all work out.

**JEAN**

Is that why you refuse to accept this?

**CONNOR**

Yes!

**JEAN**

Wouldn't it be better if you did accept it?

**CONNOR**

Better? For who?

**JEAN**

For you and for them.

**CONNOR**

No way! You're totally wrong about this.

**JEAN**

How do you know that?

3

**CONNOR**

I'm not going to accept their divorce, because it's not better or easier for anyone except you.

**JEAN**

Well, Connor, I'm not going to address that last part.

**CONNOR**

Fine.

**JEAN**

Sometimes you have to accept that certain things are beyond your control. Your parents' divorce is one of those things that's beyond you.

**CONNOR**

No, it's not.

**JEAN**

Yes, it is. What you have to do right now is to explore and deal with your feelings. Now, we can give you the emotional tools to handle the situation more effectively, but it's up to you to use them.

**CONNOR**

Can I go back to study hall?

**JEAN**

We can continue next week, but you need to think about what I've said, because events like divorces happen to us all the time in life.

**CONNOR**

They're not divorced yet!

**Connor gets up and storms out the door. Jean raises her eyebrows and scribbles in her notes.**

4

**INT. SCHOOL LIBRARY - DAY - ON CLASS** of about twenty children studying quietly. The librarian, **LINDSAY** is engrossed in 'Soap Digest.' Her appearance is frumpy, and her manner is stern. Connor enters the library. Lindsay is clearly annoyed at the interruption.

>           LINDSAY
> Connor, where have you been?

>           CONNOR
> I... uh... I... well...

>           LINDSAY
> Study hour is half over.  Where have you been?

>           CONNOR
> **(mutters)**
> I kinda had to go to the guidance office.

>           LINDSAY
> What was that you said?

The OTHER KIDS stare at Connor, making him self-conscious.

>           CONNOR
> I had to go to the guidance office.

>           LINDSAY
> Do you have a pass?

>           CONNOR
> No, I forgot.

>           LINDSAY
> Then, what were you doing **there**?

**Connor blushes as the other kids whisper.**

> LINDSAY
> Well, answer me.  Why were you there?

**Connor looks down defiantly.**

> LINDSAY
> I can call and verify, you know.

> CONNOR
> **(mutters)**
> Whatever...

> LINDSAY
> Ttcchh, don't you get smart with me young man.  You don't have a pass, and you don't have an explanation.  Maybe you need an hour of detention?

> CONNOR
> I **had** to see the counselor. Why don't you just go ahead and call?

> LINDSAY
> Ttcchh...

**Lindsay walks back to her office.**

**The kids AD LIB taunts at Connor.**

> CONNOR
> Leave me alone!

**The kid's teasing escalates.**

**Lindsay leaves her office.**

CONNOR
**(yells)**
Leave me alone!  It's none of your business!

LINDSAY
Connor, that's enough!  You now have detention all of next week
for disrupting this study hour!

**Connor's expression falls.**


**INT. CONNOR'S HOME/KITCHEN - DAY - ON MARTHA**
**As she flurries to fix a sandwich.  Martha is attractive, but**
**frazzled.  Connor enters from outdoors.  His dog, PERKY,**
**greets him enthusiastically.**

CONNOR
Hi, Mom, I'm home!

MARTHA
Hi, Connor!  Here's your sandwich and milk.  Your Dad is
supposed to come and take you to practice today.

CONNOR
Oh, yeah, I forgot...  Mom, I don't really feel like going to
practice tonight.

MARTHA
Well, you have to go.  Your dad's already on his way here. At
least he better be...

CONNOR
But Mom,...

MARTHA
We already discussed it, remember?  You need to give the team
a real try before you can just give up on it.

CONNOR

It's just, I don't feel like it today.

MARTHA

Too bad! You need a life beyond the computer. Why don't you eat your sandwich upstairs while you get all your stuff ready. Your dad will be here momentarily.

CONNOR

Awright, Mom.

**Connor exits. MIKE, Connor's father, comes into the kitchen. He looks preoccupied and serious.**


**INT. FOYER BY KITCHEN DOOR - DAY - ON CONNOR stopping to pet Perky. He hears his parents talking.**

MARTHA (O.S.)

About time you showed up.

MIKE (O.S.)

We'll make it on time. What's wrong with you?

MARTHA (O.S.)

I have to go show a house right now.

MIKE (O.S.)

Well then, go.

MARTHA (O.S.)

I guess I should be glad you showed up at all.


MIKE (O.S.)

What's that supposed to mean?

**MARTHA (O.S.)**

It means I expected you twenty minutes ago, and I never know when I can count on you. You're always busy with something more important.

**MIKE (O.S.)**

You should talk. When was the last weekend you didn't work?

**MARTHA (O.S.)**

When were you in town to notice?

**MIKE (O.S.)**

Traveling is part of my job.

**MARTHA (O.S.)**

And weekends are part of mine. That's when I make most of my money.

**Connor exits upstairs.**

**FOYER - DAY - ON CONNOR ENTERING DOWN STAIRWAY carrying his baseball gear. He stops to listen to the argument.**

**MARTHA (O.S.)**

Lunch with an associate **is** a date. We're almost divorced. You don't have to deny it anymore. I know I'm free to date now.

**MIKE (O.S.)**

If you're already seeing someone else, then I should start too, shouldn't I?

CONNOR
**(to himself)**
Oh, no!

CONNOR
**(yells)**
I'm ready!


**INT. FRONT SEAT OF CAR - DAY - ON MIKE AND CONNOR in the car going to baseball practice.**

MIKE
How was your appointment with the guidance counselor?

CONNOR
I dunno.

MIKE
You don't know or you don't want to talk about it?

CONNOR
Maybe both.

MIKE
Are you looking forward to practice?

CONNOR
I dunno.

MIKE
Your Mother really wants you to try this. A lot of boys like sports. Maybe I could pick you up at the video arcade about an hour after practice?

CONNOR

Killer!  Thanks Dad!


**EXT. BASEBALL FIELD - DAY - ON LITTLE LEAGUE TEAM practicing different drills.**

**A)  Connor strikes out.**

**B)  Connor misses a fly ball.**

**C)  Connor trips over a base.**


**EXT. BASEBALL FIELD - DAY - ON TEAM leaving the practice field.  The coach, BILL, pulls him aside.  Bill has a wholesome all-American look.**

CONNOR

Yes, Coach.


BILL

Let's talk a minute.  Ya'know Connor, there's more to sports than just playing the game.


CONNOR

Coach, it's just that...


BILL

**(continues over Connor)**

There's responsibility to the team.  They count on you. They're your friends.  You don't want to let them down, do you?


CONNOR

No, Coach.


BILL

Today, was a bad day for you, wasn't it?

11

                    CONNOR
Well, yeah, it was.

                    BILL
Once in a while, we all have a bad day.  But, you got to keep
working - keep pushing - keep trying - then it gets better.


                    CONNOR
I know, but see...

                    BILL
When you're part of a team, you gotta put your heart into it.  You
gotta practice, practice, practice.  It's dedication that pulls you
through.

                    CONNOR
Look, Coach...

                    BILL
Then a wonderful thing happens. You become a part of the team,
not just nine players, but a team.  The reward is immeasurable.
Sometimes it takes a little extra work, a few more hours of
practice, but it's well worth it.  Understand?

                    CONNOR
Yes, Coach, I understand.


**INT. ARCADE - DAY - ON SEYMOUR AND MARY
ALICE**

**SEYMOUR, the owner, and his girlfriend, MARY ALICE
are talking.  Seymour looks like a dark haired teddy bear.
Mary Alice is a flashy strawberry blonde. Connor and
BERNIE are playing video games in the b.g.**

#### MARY ALICE
See ya Saturday, Seymour?

#### SEYMOUR
Of course.  You know, Honeypie, I want to date you every Saturday night for the rest of my life.

#### MARY ALICE
You creep!

**Mary Alice pulls away and bursts into tears.**

#### MARY ALICE
You rotten creep!  I hate you!

#### SEYMOUR
What'd I say?  What'd I say?

**INT. ARCADE - DAY - ON CONNOR AND BERNIE**

**Connor is talking to BERNIE in front of Asteroids.**

#### BERNIE
Hey Connor, what's your best score in 'Asteroids'?

#### CONNOR
Twenty million, what's yours?

#### BERNIE
Twenty-two million, let's play!

CONNOR

Alright!

**The boys both rack up scores over twenty million. In the b.g. Seymour and Mary Alice argue M.O.S.**

**Bernie finishes his last turn. Connor stands at the controls. So far his score is twenty-one million.**

CONNOR

This rules! It's my best score ever!

**Connor starts to play.**

**INT. ARCADE - DAY - ON SEYMOUR AND MARY ALICE**

**Mary Alice storms toward the door.**

MARY ALICE

Damn it, Seymour! If that's the way you feel about it, then find yourself another girlfriend! Good-bye, Seymour!

SEYMOUR

What is wrong with you? Mary Alice! Get back here! Mary Alice! You can't leave like this! Mary Alice!!

**Seymour turns back and slams his fist against the wall.**

SEYMOUR

Listen up! The Arcade is closed! The Arcade is closed for the day!

**INT. ARCADE - DAY - ON CONNOR**

**Connor frantically tries to finish his game.**

      CONNOR
No, not yet!  This is the best score I've ever had!

**The power goes off.**

      SEYMOUR (O.S.)
**(bellows)**
Everybody out!  Right now!

**Connor hits the machine and lowers his head.**


**EXT. PORCH OF THE ARCADE - DAY - ON CONNOR AND PERKY dejectedly sharing an ice cream cone.**

      CONNOR
It's all wrong, Perky.  Mom and Dad belong together.  No one else even listens to me, but I'm right.

**Perky barks and takes more ice cream.  BERNIE enters, carrying a large backpack.**

      BERNIE
Hi, am I interrupting?

      CONNOR
Naw, I'm just talking to Perky.

      BERNIE
About what?

      CONNOR
My parents are getting a divorce.  I can't think about anything

else, and everything keeps going wrong.

**BERNIE**
I heard about the librarian. She's such a bitch.

**CONNOR**
Yeah, Mom is going to blow a fuse when she finds out I have detention, and it wasn't even my fault.

**BERNIE**
Yeah, maybe you should go stay with your Dad for a week or so.

**CONNOR**
I just can't deal with it anymore. My parents had a big fight today.

**BERNIE**
Bummer.

**CONNOR**
Yeah, I think they're going to start dating other people.

**BERNIE**
Cool!

**CONNOR**
What do you mean, cool?

**BERNIE**
Well, when they start dating other people, it gets their minds off of each other and they stop fighting so much. Besides, if they meet someone nice, they take you to all the really fun places.

**CONNOR**
I don't want them to get a divorce. I want them to get back together.

**BERNIE**

Well, they might. I ran into my ex-step brother the other day. His parents just got remarried.

**CONNOR**

That's great.

**BERNIE**

I don't know... He says they fight even worse now.

**CONNOR**

How did you feel when your parents got divorced?

**BERNIE**

I don't really remember. I was pretty young when they got divorced from each other. This last time my Mom got divorced, it was a relief.

**CONNOR**

They keep telling me I'll get used to it.

**BERNIE**

It has it's advantages.

**CONNOR**

Like how?

**BERNIE**

Like, you never 'didn't do' your homework. You left it at your Dad's.

**CONNOR**

Really? That works?

**BERNIE**

Sure, it works. Even better, if one parent won't let you do something, appeal to the other one. Usually they'll let you, just to get back at the first one. Another thing - they know they're traumatizing you, so they make up for it by buying a lot of new stuff for you.

CONNOR
I'd rather they got back together.

BERNIE
But, they're not going to do that.  So you might as well learn to manipulate them to get other things.

CONNOR
Manipulate?  I don't think that's right.

BERNIE
Why not?  They're yanking you around aren't they?

CONNOR
If it's so easy, could I manipulate them back together?

BERNIE
I dunno...  Why are they breaking up?

CONNOR
They're too busy for each other.  When I was little, they got along great.  Then, when Dad's book was successful, suddenly he was gone for weeks at a time.  I guess Mom got tired of waiting around, because she started selling real estate.  Since she was a really big success, she was gone all the time, too.

BERNIE
Can't they make time for each other?

CONNOR
They could, but they won't.  Mom got mad at Dad, because he was so important and gone a lot.  When Mom started working, Dad got mad at her, because she was gone a lot.  Besides, she made more money than he ever did.

**BERNIE**

So now they have tons of money, and they're spending all of it on a divorce.


**CONNOR**

Yeah, and they're mad at each other about that too.

**BERNIE**

Figures...

**CONNOR**

I just wish they'd both go back to being at home. They keep telling me it's not my fault, but no one wants to be at home with me either.

**BERNIE**

That's too bad.

**CONNOR**

I'm afraid that if they meet other people, they'll settle with someone new and never get back together.

**BERNIE**

If they're not seeing anyone now, then don't worry. If they didn't have time to see each other, they won't have time to see anyone else.

**CONNOR**

But they'll make time for someone new.

**BERNIE**

You gotta hope they meet a bunch of dorks. It's too bad you can't fix them up. Then you could be sure they only dated nerds.

**Perky barks at Connor.**

CONNOR
(to Perky)
Yeah, Perky, maybe I could.

BERNIE
How's that?

CONNOR
Perky was talking to me.

BERNIE
Oh... Okay...

**Both boys are quiet for a minute.**

CONNOR
Bernie, is there any way I can be sure they'll go out on a date?

BERNIE
Yeah, by manipulating them.

CONNOR
How?

BERNIE
Even though it's manipulating?

CONNOR
Yes, even though it's manipulating. How can I get them to go out on a date?

BERNIE
That's easy. Tell them you'll get upset if they start dating. Don't forget to sulk, then they'll buy you something really neat.

CONNOR
I guess I can try that.

**BERNIE**
But, how will that get them to only date nerds?

**CONNOR**
I still gotta work on that, but I think I can do it.

**BERNIE**
How?

**CONNOR**
I can't explain it.  I have to figure it out tonight.

**BERNIE**
So you're planning something, and you won't tell me?

**CONNOR**
I can't tell you.

**BERNIE**
That drives me crazy!  Can I come over and check it out?

**CONNOR**
Yeah.  But, first I've got to work on my parents.

**BERNIE**
Right, call me when you're done, and I'll come over.

**CONNOR**
Don't you have to ask?

**BERNIE**
No, it'll be okay.  I just talked to my Mom at the club.


**INSERT SHOT OF MIKE'S CAR PULLING UP TO ARCADE**

**BACK TO SCENE**

     CONNOR
Okay, I'll see you.

**Both boys wave as Connor exits.**

**INT. FRONT SEAT OF MOVING CAR - DAY - ON CONNOR AND MIKE**

**Connor is silent, trying his best to sulk.**

     MIKE
Was practice okay?

     CONNOR
I guess.

     MIKE
Something bothering you?

     CONNOR
Uumm...

     MIKE
Come on, Connor, what's wrong?

     CONNOR
Dad, I don't want you to date anyone except Mom.

     MIKE
Connor...

     CONNOR
Dad, why don't you and Mom get back together?

     MIKE
We explained that to you. We wanted it to work out, but it didn't.

And now it's time for each of us to go on to someone else. Neither of us like it, but that's the way it is.

**CONNOR**
Don't you still love Mom?

**MIKE**
Well, of course... But,...

**CONNOR**
Then it's wrong for you to see other women. You should stay with me and Mom.

**MIKE**
Connor, we've been through all of this before. I just don't know what more I can say to help you understand...

**CONNOR**
I'll hate them. No matter who they are, I'll hate them forever.

**MIKE**
Son, try and understand. It's time we do this. You'll get used to it. Really, you will. I'll bet a lot of your friends' parents are divorced.

**CONNOR**
They're not you.

**MIKE**
The counselor will help you understand this.

**CONNOR**
Fat chance! She's terrible!

**MIKE**
No, she's not, Connor. I'm sure she's very good.

                    CONNOR
She stinks.

                    MIKE
She does not.  You're being too hard on her.


**INSERT SHOT OF CAR PULLING UP TO HOUSE**

**BACK TO SCENE**

                    MIKE
Connor, please think this over.  It's really not so bad.

**Connor gets out of the car.  Mike is left looking troubled.**


**INT. CONNOR'S HOME/KITCHEN - DAY - ON MARTHA
as she takes a frozen dinner out of the microwave.**

                    MARTHA
Connor!  Dinner time!

**Connor enters the kitchen.**

                    CONNOR
I don't want any.

                    MARTHA
What's wrong?

                    CONNOR
Nothing.

#### MARTHA
Something's wrong.  What is it?  C'mon tell me.

#### CONNOR
Nothing.

#### MARTHA
Did you overhear your Dad and I talking?

**Connor doesn't say anything.**

#### MARTHA
He called and told me already.

**Connor still doesn't say anything.**

#### MARTHA
Connor, please try and understand.  You know your Dad and I love you.  We wouldn't hurt you for all the world, but we have to get on with our lives.

#### CONNOR
If you really loved me for all the world, you wouldn't see anyone besides Dad.

#### MARTHA
Why's that?

#### CONNOR
Cause I'll hate them, that's why.

#### MARTHA
You're being unreasonable, Connor.  How was practice?

#### CONNOR
Lousy.

MARTHA

Did the coach give you any pointers?

**Connor rolls his eyes.**

MARTHA

None of that! It's wonderful that he sacrifices his time to help you boys. You should at least appreciate that.

CONNOR

Can I go play on the computer?

MARTHA

If you take your dinner with you.

CONNOR

Okay, Mom.

MARTHA

Connor, I love you.

CONNOR

I know.


**INT. CONNOR'S BEDROOM - NIGHT - ON CONNOR AND BERNIE standing by the desk. The computer screen is covered with a pillow.**

CONNOR

You have to guess.

BERNIE

I can't guess. I don't have any idea what you're planning.

CONNOR

Try.

BERNIE

Okay... You're going to plug the computer into your parents' brains and program them to date idiots.

CONNOR

Wrong!

BERNIE

You're going to mesmerize them and feed them subliminal messages.

CONNOR

Still wrong.

BERNIE

Then what?

CONNOR

Guess.

BERNIE

I can't guess.

CONNOR

It's easy.

BERNIE

I give up. Come on, show me what you're up to.

**Connor unveils the computer screen, and Bernie stares.**

CONNOR

Ta Da!

**BERNIE**
That looks like a website!

**CONNOR**
It's going to be.

**BERNIE**
**(reads off screen)**
Nice To Meet You... Introduction Service?

**CONNOR**
I'm going to pick nerds for them to date. Want to help?

**BERNIE**
Yeah, definitely.

**CONNOR**
Great, how late can you stay?

**BERNIE**
Until whenever, I can stay over if it's okay with your mother.

**CONNOR**
Don't you have to call and ask your mother?

**BERNIE**
No, she'll figure it out. Sometimes I don't come home for a couple days. She doesn't mind.

**CONNOR**
If you disappeared altogether, would she even notice?

**BERNIE**
Oh yeah, of course. I think...

**Connor goes back to work on the computer.**

**BERNIE**

Now that you mention it, I don't know. I wonder how long it would take her to notice if I didn't come home at all.

**CONNOR**

Why don't you stay here and find out?

**BERNIE**

Won't your mother notice?

**CONNOR**

She's not home very much either. Besides, you can come in the back door.

**BERNIE**

I could get into a lot of trouble for that.

**CONNOR**

You could get in trouble! What kind of trouble do you think I'll get into?

**BERNIE**

How would they find out?

**CONNOR**

I don't know, but if they do... I'll be at least grounded forever.

**BERNIE**

But that's only if they find out. And it's only if it doesn't work...

**CONNOR**

I think they'll still be mad if they find out, even if it does work.

**BERNIE**

Yeah, but they'll get over it then, because it worked and they'll be happy about that.

#### CONNOR
Yeah, true.  Who do you think I should try to fix them up with?

#### BERNIE
Definitely fix up your dad with the librarian.  How about the gym teacher for your mother?

#### CONNOR
No, the coach!  She's always saying he's so great, but she's never really met him.

#### BERNIE
Seymour is single now.  How about him?

#### CONNOR
Perfect!  And I think Dad needs to meet the guidance counselor he sends me to.

#### BERNIE
Which one?

#### CONNOR
Jean Ellis.

#### BERNIE
Ikkk...  You really got it out for your dad.  Do you think they'll all join?

#### CONNOR
I'm saying it's a free promotional offer.  No one turns down those.

#### BERNIE
How many dates each?

#### CONNOR
I don't know...  How many people can we think of?

### BERNIE
Give them three free dates.

### CONNOR
Why?

### BERNIE
Because everything free comes in ones or threes.

### CONNOR
Right, three lousy dates might make them think more.  I need two more people...

### BERNIE
No!  Stand them up.  Someone did that to my mother once.  She was furious.

### CONNOR
Okay...  You know, this might work...


**INT. MARTHA'S OFFICE - DAY - ON MARTHA**

**Martha  checks her e-mail.  JULIE, a co-worker, enters and reads over her shoulder.**

### JULIE
Three free dates!  Lucky, you!  I didn't get one of those!

### MARTHA
I don't know if I'm interested yet.  I still have a headache from the divorce in progress.

### JULIE
I thought you just said your soon-to-be-ex- was dating someone.

### MARTHA
I don't really know that, but...

JULIE

Just don't be naive.  If he's out having fun, why should life pass
you by?  When was the last time you went out?

MARTHA

I had a bagel with my attorney last week...  You're right.  I
haven't gone out on a date in ages.

JULIE

This is what happens.  The husband winds up with a cute new
wife, because he's not sitting at home worrying about watching
the kid and paying the attorney.  Get back in the game, girl!

MARTHA

You're absolutely right.  I've got to get on with my life.  I'm
signing right up!

JULIE

That's the attitude!


**INT. MIKE'S OFFICE - DAY - ON MIKE accessing e-mail
at his desk.**

**INSERT CLOSE SHOT of computer screen showing the
'Nice To Meet You' background and logo on the screen.**


**BACK TO SCENE**


MIKE
**(mutters to himself)**
Three free dates...  Promotional offer, huh?

**Mike studies the screen.**

MIKE
(continuing)
Can't turn this down - not after that fight with Martha. If she's
going to start dating, so am I.


**INT. JEAN'S HOUSE/DEN - DAY - ON JEAN**

**Jean sets down a professional journal and checks her e-mail.**


**INSERT CLOSE SHOT of computer screen with 'Nice To
Meet You' background.**


**BACK TO SCENE as Jean thinks it over a minute, chewing
on her pencil. Then she nods happily and starts to type.**


**INT. BILL'S HOME/DEN - DAY - ON BILL watching the
ball game on television. His computer beeps. He gets up to
check his e-mail.**

BILL
Introduction service? Naww...

**Bill turns away and then shakes his head debating. Finally
he returns to the computer.**

BILL
Why not? One free date... You gotta play to win. Right?


**INT. LINDSAY'S HOUSE/LIVING ROOM - DAY - ON
LINDSAY tearfully watching the end of a soap opera. She
turns off the television and sits down at her computer.**

### LINDSAY
Promotional offer of one free date... Oh no, I couldn't... Could I...? No, no, no, no...

**She picks up her Soap Digest. It has a sexy blond woman on the cover.**

### LINDSAY
Well, Marquesa what would you do? Would you think this was foolish and dangerous? Or would you leap at the opportunity for a romantic adventure?... Yes, you would, wouldn't you?

**Lindsay focuses her attention on the computer.**

**INT. SEYMOUR'S HOUSE/REC ROOM - DAY - ON SEYMOUR as he and TWO FRIENDS are getting ready for a poker game. FIRST FRIEND is checking out the computer.**

### FIRST FRIEND
Hey! Seymour! You got e-mail.

**Seymour comes over to the computer.**

### FIRST FRIEND
Well, is it from Mary Alice?

### SEYMOUR
No, it's some stupid dating service. I can't think about anything like that right now.

### SECOND FRIEND
You ought to try it, Seymour. What do have to lose?

### SEYMOUR
No, I don't want to.

### FIRST FRIEND

Hey, it says here the first date is free! You should try it. You never know who you'll meet. Maybe they'll fix you up with Mary Alice.

### SECOND FRIEND

If nothing else, it'll get your mind off her for a while.

### FIRST FRIEND

Come on, it'll be fun. We'll help you fill out the questions so you'll get a real cool chick.

### SEYMOUR

I don't know, well... All right.


**INT. CONNOR'S BEDROOM - DAY - ON CONNOR as he enters, bursting with excitement. He throws his books on his bed and checks his computer. Happily, he raises his fist in the air.**

### CONNOR

Yesss!


**INT. MARTHA'S OFFICE - DAY - ON MARTHA as she accesses her e-mail from 'Nice To Meet You.'**

### MARTHA

Hey, Julie, c'mere!

**Julie enters.**

### JULIE

What's up?

### MARTHA

Check this out. I got e-mail from that dating service. Tell me what you think about this guy's description.

**Julie reads the screen.**

> JULIE
> Let's see here... Bill likes sports and kids - sounds like a nice guy. He teaches Social Science, so he's got an education. He wants to take you out for dinner - so go!

> MARTHA
> Yeah? You think so?

> JULIE
> Sure, why not?

> MARTHA
> It's just things with Mike and the divorce...

> JULIE
> Last week you said all the terms were settled and nothing was left but signatures and attorneys' bills. Are you having second thoughts?

> MARTHA
> No, not about that. I just haven't dated in a long time. I feel strange about it.

> JULIE
> Come on, take the plunge. It's only dinner. This guy sounds nice.

> MARTHA
> You're right. I can clear out early on Wednesday. Connor can spend the evening with Mike.

**INT. MIKE'S OFFICE - DAY - ON MIKE** sitting at his computer.

**INSERT CLOSE SHOT of the computer screen showing the 'Nice To Meet You' background.**

**BACK TO SCENE as JEFF enters the office.**

>            JEFF
> Hey, Mike, are you going to McCulley's seminar on Tuesday evening?

>            MIKE
> **(still reading e-mail)**
> No, I can't.  I think I have a date.

>            JEFF
> Really?

>            MIKE
> Maybe...  You're single.  Take a look and tell me what you think.

**Jeff reads over his shoulder.**

>            JEFF
> Sounds pretty enough.  She has a degree in counseling and in education.  Have you talked to her?

>            MIKE
> No, why?

>            JEFF
> Personally, I like to meet them first, but I've been single a long time.

### MIKE
She wants me to meet her at a coffee bar. Maybe I should find out more about her.

### JEFF
I take it the divorce is all over with?

### MIKE
All except the bills and actual legalities. I've accepted it, if that's what you mean.

### JEFF
Then, jump on in. This Jean sounds as nice as anyone else. Too bad they don't have photos.

### MIKE
True...


**INT. O'LEARY'S PUB - NIGHT - ON MARTHA AND BILL sitting at a table. The pub has sports decor and several television sets with a baseball game on.**

### BILL
So, you're Martie.

### MARTHA
Martha, yes, that's right.

### BILL
This is my favorite little neighborhood restaurant. Everything on the menu is good, especially the pasta and the meat loaf.

### MARTHA
It's cute.

BILL

So, Martie, the Yankees are at Fenway tonight.   You like baseball, don't you?

**Martha winces at the nickname.**

MARTHA

It's okay.  Are you a big fan?

BILL

The greatest!  I love sports.

MARTHA

Which ones?

BILL

All of 'em.  Either I'm watching or playing or coaching a Little League team.

MARTHA

My son, Connor is in Little League.

BILL

Connor, yeh, I know Connor.  Hey, that kid needs to get some serious practice time in.   He's a nice kid, but he's all butterfingers.

MARTHA

Well, he has other talents.

BILL

Sure, sure he does, but you gotta have sports.

**The WAITRESS enters.**

WAITRESS

Can I get you some drinks?

MARTHA

Do you have a nice Chablis?

WAITRESS

Is house white okay?  I think it's a Chablis.

MARTHA

Do you have a wine list?

WAITRESS

Umm, no.

MARTHA

House white will be fine.

BILL

I'll have my usual.

WAITRESS

Okay, a house white and a Bud Lite.  Tonight's special is swordfish and pasta.

**WAITRESS exits.**

BILL

Martie, what about you.  What do you like to do?

MARTHA

Well, I sell real estate. I started part-time a few years ago, and I really enjoy it.

BILL

That's important.

**Bill glances at the television behind her.  WAITRESS enters with their drinks.**

WAITRESS

Can I take your dinner order?

> ### MARTHA
> I'll have the special.  I love swordfish.

> ### BILL
> Nothing fancy for me.  I want a steak with onions and fries. Medium rare.

> ### WAITRESS
> Anything else?

**WAITRESS exits.**

> ### MARTHA
> My degree is in Greek literature.  I taught Greek for a while. Then when Connor was little, I stayed home with him.

> ### BILL
> Yeh, that's important for a kid.

**Bill surreptitiously watches the television.**

> ### MARTHA
> As he got older, I wanted to get back to my career, but there's not much call for Greek in the suburbs. I really felt I needed to do something besides be...

> ### BILL
> GO!  GO!  GO!!

**Bill stands up cheering.**

> ### BILL
> Come on!  Come on!  Yes!  YES!!!

**Bill sits down again.**

BILL
**(continuing)**
Did you see that!  What a play!!!

MARTHA
Uh, no...  I...

BILL
That was excellent.  What a throw!  Ah, man, what a throw!
Now what were you saying?

MARTHA
I was telling you about how I got started in real estate.

BILL
Yeah, yeah, go on about that.

MARTHA
Although my degree still gave me a sense of identity, I felt I
needed to...

BILL
What was your degree in?

MARTHA
Greek literature.

BILL
Oh, which sorority?

MARTHA
No, that's different.

BILL
Well, you said Greek, so I thought...

                    MARTHA

No, this was the literature and language of Greece.

                    BILL

Oh, yeah, I was thinking of something else.  That sounds like a
difficult major.

**Bill returns to glancing at the television.**

                    MARTHA

Challenging was the word they sold us on.

**Martha sees that Bill is still watching the game.**

                    MARTHA
**(continuing)**
Would you prefer to watch the game?

                    BILL

No, no, of course not.  I'm taping it at home.  Tell me about your
career.


                    MARTHA

Well, when I first started at the real estate office...

                    BILL
YEAH!  Awright!

**Martha sighs.**


**INT. COFFEE JAR CAFE - NIGHT - ON JEAN as she sits
down at a table with Mike.  The Coffee Jar is trendy but
casual.**

MIKE
Yes, I'm Mike.

JEAN
Nice to meet you - oh!  Ha-ha! I didn't mean that.

**Mike smiles awkwardly.**

JEAN
**(continuing)**
This is one of my favorite places.  The cappuccino is just wonderful.

MIKE
It looks...  interesting.

JEAN
You're recently separated?

MIKE
Well, yes, this is my first date in a - a long time.

JEAN
Yes, I could tell by your body language.

MIKE
I really don't go to this kind of place much.  Do they serve coffee with liqueurs?

JEAN
No, no alcohol, just coffees and teas.

MIKE
Oh, that's too bad.  Is cappuccino their specialty?

JEAN
Um-hmm...

**WAITRESS enters.**

WAITRESS
What can I get you?

JEAN
Two cappuccino and a plate of pizzelles.

MIKE
What are pizzelles?

JEAN
They're Italian cookies.

WAITRESS
An anise flavored Mediterranean pastry.

MIKE
Then by all means.  I spend a lot of time in the Mediterranean area.

**Waitress exits.**

JEAN
What for?

MIKE
I'm a historian.  I specialize in Ottoman artwork, so I spend a lot of time in Turkey.

JEAN
Is that near the Mediterranean?

MIKE
Aahh, yes...  What do you do?

JEAN

Counseling.  I counsel privately, and I'm a guidance counselor at the middle school.

MIKE

Then this is embarrassing.  I think you've probably seen my son Connor.

JEAN

Oh, he's a very nice boy.

**Mike looks uncomfortable.**

JEAN

You're so recently separated. How do you feel about dating at this point in your process?

MIKE

Process?

JEAN

The process of separation, divorce, and re-establishment of the single identity.

MIKE

Un-huh...

JEAN

You realize the identity has to re-emerge during the separation phase?

MIKE

Unn-huhn.

JEAN

So, what are your feelings at this phase?

MIKE

I'd really rather keep this conversation light.


JEAN

Un-huh...

**The WAITRESS enters with the order.**
**Mike tries a pizzelle.**

MIKE

I think I had these in Greece on my... uh... vacation.


JEAN

You're hiding something.


MIKE

It was my honeymoon, but I thought it was inappropriate to mention that.


JEAN

Are you repressing feeling about your marriage?


MIKE

I just don't want to discuss it with you.


JEAN

Do you think being distant affected your marriage?


MIKE

You mean the traveling?


JEAN

I meant emotionally, but it's interesting you bring up a physical manifestation.


MIKE

I didn't come here for a therapy session, just a date.

JEAN
Un-huh.

MIKE
I still have to finish up some work tonight.

JEAN
Do you frequently deal with your problems this way?

**Mike downs his coffee and stands up to leave.**

MIKE
Yes.

**Mike exits resolutely.**


**INT. MARTHA'S OFFICE - DAY - ON MARTHA  sitting at her desk, hanging up the phone.**

MARTHA
Hey, Julie, can I have the keys to that new four bed on Linden Avenue?

JULIE (O.S.)
I'll be right there.

**Martha turns to the computer and the 'Nice To Meet You' background appears on the screen.**
**Julie enters and stands next to her desk.**

JULIE
I've got the keys.

MARTHA
Good, can I have them for the afternoon?

JULIE

No.

MARTHA

Is someone else showing it?

JULIE

No.

MARTHA

Then why can't I have them?

JULIE

Because you haven't told me about your date yet.

**They both laugh.**

MARTHA

You and the dating service… They want to know too.

JULIE

Well...

MARTHA

Well, it was okay, sort of.

JULIE

Where'd you go?

MARTHA

To a pub - sports bar kind of place.  It was nice.

JULIE

Not great?

MARTHA

I don't think he listened to a word I said.

JULIE
Why's that?


MARTHA
Because he kept interrupting me to cheer his team on.


JULIE
Oh, men are like that...  Was he good looking?


MARTHA
Yeah, he was, I guess.


JULIE
Then get to know him better.


MARTHA
I think I got to know him well enough.  Being ignored wasn't fun.  I don't know how other women stand it.


JULIE
You've got to compromise somewhere or be all alone.


MARTHA
Still...  Even Connor doesn't like him.


JULIE
Connor knows him?


MARTHA
Bill coaches Little League.  I guess Connor can't deal with his obsession either.


JULIE
Oh, come on, he can't be that bad.


MARTHA
He's not.  When you get right down to it, I have so much to do in life that I feel like I wasted a precious evening with a jerk.

JULIE

The next one will be better. Just tell the dating service what you want.


**INT. MIKE'S OFFICE - DAY - ON MIKE AND JEFF sitting in Mike's office. Mike look tired and studies his cup of coffee.**

JEFF

Are you drinking that coffee or are you trying to memorize it?

MIKE

I'm just tired. I couldn't sleep, because I drank a cup of coffee last night. I'm debating about drinking more. It might not be a good idea.

JEFF

Why were you drinking coffee at night?

MIKE

Well... You remember that computer date? We went to a place that only had coffee.

JEFF

So... Was it the coffee that kept you awake? Or was it something else?

MIKE

It wasn't my date. She was awful. She didn't stop counseling for a minute, and she was snide about it, too.

JEFF

Did you get anything out of the session?

MIKE

Very funny. I've chalked the whole thing up to a freak bad

experience. I already gave the dating service an ear full. The only thing that bothers me is Connor.

JEFF
Connor? Your son? What's he got to do with it?

MIKE
Jean is Connor's guidance counselor at school. He's still not accepting the divorce, so I sent him to see her. He told me she was terrible. I thought he was exaggerating.

JEFF
Then before you do anything else, cancel his appointment with her. Women can be very vindictive, take it from a single man.

MIKE
Funny, I noticed that same thing while we were working out our divorce.

JEFF
Okay, call the school, drink the coffee, and come by my office when you're ready to work.

MIKE
Alright, see you in a few.

**EXT. CONNOR'S BACK YARD - DAY - ON CONNOR AND BERNIE sitting on the lawn, eating potato chips and feeding some to Perky.**

CONNOR

So far things are going great!  Both Mom and Dad had a crummy time.  Dad hated Miss Ellis.  He said she was snide and condescending.  He didn't get any sleep because he drank cappuccino, so he was really grouchy.

BERNIE

She is snide and condescending.  What did your Mom think of Coach?

CONNOR

Not very much.  He ignored her and watched the ball game.

BERNIE

Figures...  You know, I was thinking about what you said about my Mom last week.  All week, I've been at home, and she hasn't even noticed me.  Maybe she wouldn't mind if I disappeared altogether.

CONNOR

No, she's probably just busy this week.  I'm sure she'd miss you eventually.

BERNIE

I wonder when, but I'm kind of afraid to find out.

CONNOR

She might not notice you when you're there, but I bet if you weren't there at all she'd notice.

BERNIE

I think I will hide out here for a while and test it out.

### CONNOR
You're sure she won't notice when you don't come home tonight?

### BERNIE
No, she'll just figure I'm at my dad's.

### CONNOR
Won't she call him?

### BERNIE
No, they're really hostile right now, because his support checks have been bouncing.

### CONNOR
You can hang out here until my mother gets wise.

### BERNIE
Cool, I'll go home tonight and get some of my stuff.

### CONNOR
Want some more chips?

### BERNIE
Sure.

**Perky barks.**

### CONNOR
Okay, Perk, you can have some too.

**Connor tears open the bag. Both boys and Perky eat some more.**

**BERNIE**

So, who're you going to fix them up with next?

**CONNOR**

I want Mom to go out with Seymour before he makes up with Mary Alice.

**BERNIE**

How're you going to get her to do that?

**CONNOR**

I'm telling her he's an entrepreneur with his own business. That sounds pretty impressive.

**BERNIE**

Yeah, that'll work. What about your dad?

**CONNOR**

I set him up with Miss McCray. I hope she likes to drink wine.

**BERNIE**

Why's that?

**CONNOR**

I said she appreciated fine wines and dining, because I know my Dad does.

**BERNIE**

Well, really, if she doesn't, so much the better. Did you say what they looked like?

**CONNOR**

Sort of, I made them sound a little better than they are.

**BERNIE**

That's probably what they would have done.

                    CONNOR

That's what I figured.  We're out of potato chips.  Let's go get
some more.


**INT. GUIDANCE OFFICE - DAY - ON JEAN at her desk.**

**Connor enters Jean's office.**

                    JEAN

Hello, Connor.  I got a call from your father this morning. You
don't need to come here for visits anymore.  But, since you're
here, do you mind answering a few questions?

                    CONNOR

Like what?

                    JEAN

Would you say your father is a cold man?  Does he often hold in
his emotions?

**Connor doesn't say anything.**

                    JEAN

How do you deal with his example?

                    CONNOR

My Dad said I don't have to come here anymore, right?

                    JEAN

That's correct.

                    CONNOR

Then I'm going to study hall before I'm late.

**Connor exits quickly.  Jean sighs with a petulant frown.**

**INT. MIKE'S CAR - DAY - ON MIKE AND CONNOR as Mike drives Connor to practice.**

> CONNOR
>
> Hi, Dad!

> MIKE
>
> Hi, Connor. How was school?

> CONNOR
>
> It was good. Thanks for getting me out of those counseling appointments.

> MIKE
>
> I don't have a lot of faith in that stuff.

> CONNOR
>
> It only made me feel worse anyways.

> MIKE
>
> We'll get through it together, Connor. It'll get better. How was school otherwise?

> CONNOR
>
> It was fine. Nothing special happened.

**EXT. BASEBALL FIELD - DAY - ON TEAM having batting practice. Connor is the last one up.**

> BILL
>
> Alright! Connor, you're up! This is the last round. Give it what you got!

**Connor tries hard, but he still strikes out.**
**The TEAM sneers.**

BILL

Okay, Team!  That's it for the day, boys.  You all did great!

**The TEAM start to disperse.  Bill motions Connor aside.**


**EXT.  BASEBALL  FIELD  -  DAY  -  ON  BILL  AND CONNOR**

BILL

Hey, you improved this week, Connor.

CONNOR

Thanks Coach.

BILL

Did you get in any practice at home?

CONNOR

Well, not really.

BILL

Practice is important.  Are either of your parents interested in sports?

CONNOR

Hunh-unnh.

BILL

Does your Dad play any sports?

CONNOR

No.

BILL

How about your Mom?

**CONNOR**

No.

**BILL**

Nothing?  She doesn't like basketbball or hockey?

**CONNOR**

Not really.

**BILL**

How about tennis or golf?

**CONNOR**

No.

**BILL**

That makes it tough to get enthused doesn't it?

**CONNOR**

Yeah, I guess so.

**BILL**

It's hard to enjoy something when you aren't good at it yet.  It makes you feel self-conscious doesn't it?

**CONNOR**

Yeah, it does.

**BILL**

Listen, I was thinking.  There's a couple other boys on the team like you.  They don't get a lot of support at home.  Maybe we could all get together for an optional practice sometimes?  We could work on some of the trouble spots and smooth them out. What do you think of that?

**CONNOR**

That'd be great, Coach.

**INT. RESTAURANT - NIGHT - ON LINDSAY AND MIKE seated at a table with a bottle of wine. The restaurant has a French country atmosphere.**

      MIKE
Do you like the Chablis?

      LINDSAY
Oh, yes.

      MIKE
This particular vintage is pretty versatile.

      LINDSAY
It's lovely!  I like wine, but I never order a bottle with dinner. This is a real treat for me.

**Lindsay drinks quite a bit.**

      MIKE
I'm glad you like it.

      LINDSAY
Mike, what do you do?

      MIKE
I'm a historian.  I specialize in the Ottoman Empire.

      LINDSAY
Fascinating!

      MIKE
I do a lot of lecturing and research at this point.  In a couple of years I'm planning on revising my textbook, but I'm called in to authenticate relics so frequently it may be a while until I get to it.

LINDSAY
What kind of relics?

MIKE
Mostly artwork.  What do you do?

LINDSAY
Well, I'm a librarian.

MIKE
Which library do you work at?

LINDSAY
I work at two places part-time, the public library and the middle school library in town.

MIKE
My son, Connor goes to middle school.

**Lindsay drinks heavily and blushes with guilt.**

LINDSAY
I can't really place him. Have you been separated long?

MIKE
Long enough.  You're...?

LINDSAY
Divorced.

**Lindsay finishes her glass and pours another.  She is tipsy.**

LINDSAY
It was a mistake from the very beginning.  Dating Eddie was fun, but while we walked down the aisle, I started feeling distant.  We just never had anything together.  Oh, you know how it is.  I'm sure you feel the same way about your ex-.

**Mike disagrees, but doesn't answer.**

> LINDSAY
>
> I thought it would be like on the soaps. I wanted undying passion and romance. I got a lump who liked frozen dinners and sit-coms.

> MIKE
>
> That's really too bad...

> LINDSAY
>
> I still hope for it.

> MIKE
>
> For what?

> LINDSAY
>
> Undying passion and romance. Every time I see Rutherford and Sioban rekindle their love, I hope someday I'll have that kind of relationship.

**The WAITER brings their dinner.**

> MIKE
>
> Who are Rutherford and Sioban?

> LINDSAY
>
> Rutherford is the illegitimate son of the wealthiest man in 'Elliot Place.' Sioban is only the maid, so he'll be disinherited if he marries her. I watch them faithfully everyday at four o'clock.

> MIKE
>
> They're not real?

> LINDSAY
>
> No.

**There's an uncomfortable silence as they eat and drink.**

**Lindsay is drunk.**

#### LINDSAY
Why don't you tell me about your work.  Do you travel a lot?

#### MIKE
Yes, quite a bit.  I spend a lot of time in the Mediterranean basin, particularly Turkey as you might expect.

#### LINDSAY
Ohhh, that's so exciting!

#### MIKE
Of course, it's not all exciting.  I also spend a lot of time lecturing in the United States.

#### LINDSAY
That's still exciting!

#### MIKE
I guess it wears off after a while.  My wife always complained about it.

#### LINDSAY
I would love it!  I'd go everywhere with you.  The world would be our playground.

#### MIKE
You wouldn't want to be home or even have a home?

#### LINDSAY
Oh no, I can't be home without you.  I'm sure I'll develop a drinking problem just like poor Glenda.  No, I'll have to be your constant companion.

MIKE
Ah, you're getting ahead of...


LINDSAY
We'll live like Gypsies... Just like Tad and Terra do.


MIKE
Tad and...


LINDSAY
He swept her off her feet. They left the show and ran away to South America together. God knows where they are now.


MIKE
Un-huh...


**INT. RESTAURANT - NIGHT - ON MARTHA AND SEYMOUR seated in a romantic Italian restaurant. There's already a bottle of wine on the table. Seymour is pouring.**

SEYMOUR
Pasta and Chianti, I just love pasta and Chianti. That's my idea of a real meal.


MARTHA
I enjoy wine with dinner. I think it adds a touch of elegance that's missing otherwise.


SEYMOUR
Mary Alice always liked Chianti, too.


MARTHA
Is Mary Alice your ex-?

### SEYMOUR

Sort of. Until last week she was my girl. I don't want to talk about Mary Alice right now. Let's talk about you. What do you do?

### MARTHA

I sell real estate. I started a few years ago, just part time. Now I'm on the run with it all the time. I just love it, and of course the money is nice for a change.

### SEYMOUR

Business is really what it's all about in life. That's why I didn't waste a real lot of time on college. I took a couple of business classes, and I'm doing great.

**Martha doesn't agree with this, but she keeps it to herself.**

### MARTHA

What business are you in?

### SEYMOUR

I own the a video arcade by the park. It's a great business - low overhead and excellent return. Besides, it gives the kids something wholesome to do.

### MARTHA

My son, Connor, just loves the arcade. I bet you know him. He's eleven, and he has auburn hair.

**Seymour hesitates guiltily.**

### SEYMOUR

I can't place him, but I'd know him if I saw him. I love having the kids around. Of course, Mary Alice was always complaining. She said I never had time for her, because I worked a lot of evenings and weekends. But that's part of being an entrepreneur. Being in real estate, I'm sure you understand that.

### MARTHA

Oh, yes, you have to be available when your customers have
time. My husband never understood either, but then, he didn't
consider making money very important.

### SEYMOUR

Yeah, what's he do?

### MARTHA

He's a historian specializing in the Ottoman Empire.

### SEYMOUR

Yeah? Sounds real intellectual.

### MARTHA

He is.

### SEYMOUR

You'd think all those smart people would understand about
making a living. I remember when Mary Alice was in school -
study, study, study. You know what ridiculous thing she wasted
her money on? A course in Greek history. Can you imagine
that?

**The Waiter enters in the b.g. with their dinners.**
**Martha blushes and opens her mouth to reply.**
**The Waiter interrupts by bringing their dinners.**

### SEYMOUR

Doesn't this look great? Try your pasta.

### MARTHA

It's delicious. Thanks for suggesting it.

### SEYMOUR

We used to get that dish a lot, me and...

#### MARTHA
Mary Alice?

#### SEYMOUR
I'm sorry, but I can't get her off my mind. She was my girl for two years. We were so happy together... Now she won't even speak to me. I know I keep talking about her, but I can't think about anything else.

#### MARTHA
Well, I know how it is. I caught myself thinking Mike would like this place.

#### SEYMOUR
I'm all torn up inside because of Mary Alice. You're really nice. I mean that, you're a sweet person.

#### MARTHA
Thanks, Seymour.

#### SEYMOUR
You know the worst part? I don't even know what I said wrong. I'm being sweet, and she starts crying and yelling at me. She won't even tell me why.

#### MARTHA
What did you say to her?

#### SEYMOUR
I was being real lovey-dovey. We see each other every Saturday night, no matter what. I told her I wanted to date her every Saturday night for the rest of my life, and she got mad at me. I don't get it. I mean would you be mad if I said that to you?

#### MARTHA
Propose.

### SEYMOUR
What?

### MARTHA
Propose.  Ask her to marry you.

### SEYMOUR
Yeah?  You think so?

### MARTHA
Do you love her?  Do you want to be your girl forever?  Then what're you waiting for?

### SEYMOUR
How am I going to ask her?  She won't even talk to me.

### MARTHA
She will if you send her a diamond ring first, especially if it's a very large diamond.

### SEYMOUR
You really think so?  That's what's bothering her?  She threw a fit, because she wants to get married?

### MARTHA
Of course she does!  No one wants to just date forever. Everyone wants to have someone with them all the time, not just a couple of evenings a week.

### SEYMOUR
Yeah, you're right.  I never thought about it before.  That'd be great!  I'll be with Mary Alice all the time.  I'm gonna do that. First thing tomorrow, I'm picking out a ring for her.

### MARTHA
Well, good, let me know how it all works out.

SEYMOUR
So, how big a diamond should I get?


**INT. MARTHA'S OFFICE - DAY - ON MARTHA AND JULIE seated at the desk. Julie is looking at the computer.**

MARTHA
What do you think of that response? Is it too scathing?

JULIE
Maybe a bit. It isn't the dating service's fault he's in love with someone else.

MARTHA
But why would they fix me up with someone who felt like that? It's totally inappropriate.

JULIE
Maybe the service didn't know. Also the rebound is sometimes an excellent time to meet.

MARTHA
You're right. I'm stressed, because I wasted another evening. You know last night, I rescheduled an appointment that could've sold a house. I dropped off my poor son like a UPS parcel. And why did I do this? To listen to some guy cry about his girlfriend?

JULIE
Take it easy, you're blowing this out of proportion. You always need a certain amount of time for yourself. Connor will be okay with it. These last two dates were just bad luck. You don't expect every person you show a house to to buy it, do you?

MARTHA
That's all true...

JULIE

If you don't date now, when will you start? It only gets harder. Believe me, because I waited, and it was a mistake.

MARTHA

You really think this is just bad luck?

JULIE

You want another sweetie, right? Well, this is how you meet them... Be patient. You'll get used to the single parent thing and so will Connor.


**INT. MIKE'S OFFICE - DAY - ON MIKE AND JEFF eating lunch.**

MIKE

She was unbelievable - a textbook case of schizophrenia.

JEFF

No, get out of here...

MIKE

I mean it. She spoke very emotionally about all these fictional people.

JEFF

Are you sure they're fiction?

MIKE

Yes, she said they were on her soap operas.

JEFF
**(laughing)**
They're all like that. Get used to it.

MIKE

What? Who?

JEFF

Women who watch soaps.  They all think the characters are real.

MIKE

You're kidding...

JEFF

No, my ex-sister-in-law canceled her second honeymoon, because she had to see if Giselle was really alive.

MIKE

Who's Giselle?

JEFF

Who cares?  Tell the dating service two thumbs down, and chalk it all up to experience.

MIKE

Yeah, I'll do that.


**INT. CONNOR'S BEDROOM - DAY - ON CONNOR AND BERNIE playing a computer game.**

BERNIE

Awwww!  I'm dead!

CONNOR

All right!  I won after all. I got worried when you got to that last level.

BERNIE

I never got that far before. How do you avoid those red spaceships?

**CONNOR**

You've got to duck under the buildings real fast. Let me check out my e-mail.

**BERNIE**

Did your parents have any dates last night?

**CONNOR**

Yeah, I should be getting some feedback from them here... Great! Neither of them had any fun.

**BERNIE**

Good! What do they say?

**CONNOR**

Mom said Seymour was an inappropriate match for her, because he's in madly in love with someone else.

**BERNIE**

I guess he's still moping over Mary Alice. That's too bad, he's really a pretty nice guy.

**CONNOR**

Don't forget, the idea is for them not to get along.

**BERNIE**

That's right.

**CONNOR**

Dad thinks Miss McCray is a psycho.

**BERNIE**

That's great! So what next? Are you still going to stand them both up, and then get them back together?

**CONNOR**

Better, I've decided to stand both of them up at the same place and time.

BERNIE

So that when the expected dates don't show up, they'll see each other, right?

CONNOR

Exactly! Think it'll work?

BERNIE

Maybe. At least it's going better than my plan's going.

CONNOR

How long since you've been home?

BERNIE

Well, I was gone almost all week, but I got caught picking up my favorite CD last night. Since I was there, I thought I might as well stay. So I've really just started over again today.

CONNOR

Better luck this week.


**INT. BROWNLEY'S KITCHEN - DAY - ON MARTHA as Connor enters.**

CONNOR

Hi, Mom, I'm home.

MARTHA

Connor, I want to talk to you!

CONNOR

What is it, Mom?

MARTHA

Young man, you are in trouble! Now, I don't want to hear about how you're upset about the divorce.  There is no excuse for this!

### CONNOR
But, Mom, can't you understand...

### MARTHA
Understand what?  I will not tolerate this kind of behavior under any circumstances, and I'm sure your father will agree with me.

### CONNOR
I thought you and Dad would understand when...

### MARTHA
Understand what?  The principal said you have detention for a week because you caused a disruption in the library!

### CONNOR
That?  That wasn't my fault...

### MARTHA
Your father's calling me back. Now, why would you do something like that?

### CONNOR
Mom, it wasn't like they say...

**The TELEPHONE RINGS and Martha answers it.**

### MARTHA
**(on telephone)**
Hello, Mike, it's about Connor. He has detention all week next week...  He caused a disruption in the library, so the librarian... Yes, it was definitely the librarian...  Well, I'm not sure...  Well, all right, if you think the detention itself is adequate...  In that case, it's okay with me. By the way, could Connor stay with you on Tuesday evening?

CONNOR
**(to himself)**
Oh, no... I didn't think about this...

MARTHA
**(on telephone)**
No, it's not a problem... I don't know why I thought you'd help anyway... I have to go... Good-bye.

MARTHA
**(to Connor)**
Connor, your Dad thinks the detention itself is punishment enough. I'm not so sure, but I'll let it drop as long as it doesn't happen again. Understood?

CONNOR
Yes, Mom. Mom, on Tuesday evening can I go to Bernie's? I want to check out his new computer game.

MARTHA
Tuesday...? Yes, that would be alright.


**INT. ELEGANT RESTAURANT - NIGHT - ON MIKE waiting in the front of the restaurant. He sees Martha entering.**

**A) Mike quickly exits into the bar.**

**B) Martha enters from the front door looking around.**

**C) Martha peers tentatively into the bar.**

**D) Martha steps back quickly.**

**E) Martha sits down on a chair in the front.**

**F) Mike enters the doorway of the bar to look out.**

G) Martha quickly turns away.

H) Mike spots her and exits into the bar.

I) Martha gets up and looks around again.

J) Martha goes back to her chair and turns around.

K) Mike cautiously enters the doorway of the bar.

L) Mike crosses the room behind Martha.

M) Mike exits into the restaurant.

N) Martha checks her watch.

O) Martha looks into the bar.

P) Martha exits into the bar.

Q) Martha enters from the bar.

R) Martha returns to her chair.

S) Mike enters behind her from the restaurant.

T) Mike exits into the bar.

U) Martha paces, then exits through the front door.

V) Mike enters from the bar.

W) Mike waits a minute, checking his watch.

X) Mike exits through the front door.

**INT. MARTHA'S OFFICE - DAY - ON MARTHA AND
JULIE talking over coffee.**

> MARTHA
>
> That's right, stood up!  It was incredibly embarrassing!

> JULIE
>
> You shouldn't be embarrassed. It happens to all of us.

> MARTHA
>
> With their almost ex- husband there?   When I saw Mike, I
> wanted to die!  I just pray he didn't see me.

> JULIE
>
> Oh, no!  That is really awful! But, I'm sure there's a good reason
> this guy stood you up.  Did you call the service?

> MARTHA
>
> I left an e-mail.

> JULIE
>
> I hope you demanded another date from them.

> MARTHA
>
> What for?  I don't want to meet this guy.

> JULIE
>
> They owe you!

> MARTHA
>
> They do owe me, but all this has done is make me feel worse.
> Now I feel either I'm not worth meeting, or else they're not worth
> meeting.

> JULIE
>
> The third time's the charm.

MARTHA
It's also the last time.


**INT. MIKE'S OFFICE - DAY - ON MIKE AND JEFF
seated and looking over paperwork.**

MIKE
I had time to finish the syllabus last night after all.

JEFF
I thought you had another date last night.

MIKE
I did, but she stood me up.

JEFF
That's too bad.

MIKE
It was almost worse. Martha was at the same place waiting for someone.

JEFF
No! Did she see you?

MIKE
I don't think so. She was looking the other way.

JEFF
That's good. What a terrible coincidence.

MIKE
I guess I've had an unusual run of bad luck. None of my three dates panned out.

JEFF
That's not unusual.

MIKE

No?

JEFF

No, not at all.  Hardly anyone you meet works out.

MIKE

I just meant a nice evening...

JEFF

Look, out of ten blind dates, if two or three are tolerable, you're doing well.  Your dates are pretty typical of what's out there.

MIKE

Seriously?  They're all like this?

JEFF

Seriously, no.  Some are worse.

MIKE

I never knew you felt that way.

JEFF

The grass is always greener isn't it?

MIKE

Yeah, I guess so...


**INT. CONNOR'S BEDROOM - NIGHT - ON CONNOR AND BERNIE sitting by the computer with Perky.  Bernie is reading the screen.**

CONNOR

See for yourself - it didn't work at all.  They didn't even talk to each other.  Mom has been in a terrible mood all day.

**BERNIE**

Yeah, you're right...  Look it didn't work, but your dad says here he demands another date.

**CONNOR**

Who am I going to fix him up with now?

**BERNIE**

I don't know.  It's not like he can demand his money back.

**CONNOR**

I really want him to see Mom right now.

**BERNIE**

So, set the two of them up together.

**CONNOR**

No way, they'll know it's each other.

**BERNIE**

Change their names a little bit.  Say Mike is Miguel...

**CONNOR**

Yeah...  Yeah, Martha could be Martina.

**BERNIE**

That's a hot name.  I'm sure they'd both go for that.

**CONNOR**

They'd both go, but they might see each other and leave.

**BERNIE**

Oh yeah...  How about if you leave special instructions with the reservations.  At least, that should get them curious.

**CONNOR**

I can order anything on the computer, but Dad will get the bill.

**BERNIE**
Then, you're caught for sure.

**CONNOR**
I'll be in big trouble with both of them if that happens.

**BERNIE**
Maybe not... I'm not in any trouble yet, and you said I'd be in serious trouble last week.

**CONNOR**
That's true, but you've been going to school and e-mailing your dad, so they know you're not dead or anything.

**BERNIE**
My dad wouldn't be looking for me anyway. He lets my mother keep track of me.

**CONNOR**
How long since they've seen you?

**BERNIE**
Not quite a week, but the point is, I'm not in any trouble yet.

**CONNOR**
Are you going to keep doing this until you are?

**BERNIE**
Or until I get tired of it, which ever comes first.

**CONNOR**
I'm going to do it!

**Perky yips.**

**CONNOR**
Yeah!

**BERNIE**
What?

**CONNOR**
I'm going to go for it.  I'm fixing up my parents.  I'm ordering flowers and candles and a secluded table.

**BERNIE**
What about getting caught?

**CONNOR**
I've got to do it.  They're almost back together.  I can feel it.

**BERNIE**
Yeah, and what can they do to you anyway?

**CONNOR**
I could be grounded.  They could take away the computer.

**BERNIE**
That would stink!

**CONNOR**
It would, but I use it for my homework, so they'd eventually give it back.

**BERNIE**
Are you too old for spanking?

**CONNOR**
I hope so...  You know, I'm already miserable.  If there's even a chance this will work, it's worth being punished.  I have to try it and just hope they don't get too mad at me.

**BERNIE**
Okay...  What do Miguel and Martina do for a living?

**INT. FOYER OF BROWNLEY HOME - DAY - ON MARTHA waiting at the bottom of the stairs. Connor is coming down the stairway dressed for school.**

> MARTHA

Connor, are you all ready to go?

> CONNOR

Yeah.

> MARTHA

On Thursday night, Maureen is going to be here with you.

> CONNOR

Where are you going to be?

> MARTHA

That's not anything you need to be concerned with young man.

> CONNOR

Yes it is! You're my Mom!

> MARTHA

And because I'm your mother, you should do what I say.

> CONNOR

Mom!! Where are you going? It's not a date is it, Mom? I don't want you to date. I want you to get back with Dad!

> MARTHA

Not another word from you, or you don't go to the arcade for a month. Now off to school before you're late.

**Martha walks Connor to the door.**

> CONNOR

What about Dad? Why can't I stay with Dad? I haven't seen him all week.

### MARTHA
Because you can't, but if you're good now, you can go to the arcade tonight. How's that for a deal?

### CONNOR
Aawww Mom....! All right.

**(EXT. NEIGHBORHOOD SIDEWALK - DAY - ON CONNOR grudgingly leaving the house. As he gets out of sight, he jumps and waves his fist in the air triumphantly.**

### CONNOR
YES!

**INT. ARCADE - DAY - ON SEYMOUR AND MARY ALICE kissing by the doorway. Mary Alice is wearing a sparkling engagement ring. Connor is standing at a machine in the b.g.**

### MARY ALICE
See you tonight, Honeybun.

### SEYMOUR
I love you, Sweetheart. See you tonight.

**Mary Alice exits.**
**Seymour notices Connor.**

### SEYMOUR
Hey, kid, are you Connor Brownley?

### CONNOR
Yeah.

                    SEYMOUR
Come here kid, I got something for you.

**Seymour digs into his pocket and pulls out a roll of 'Free Game' tokens.**

                    SEYMOUR
You know, your mom's a real classy lady, and I got a lot to thank her for.  Now you take these and have lots of fun.

**Seymour hands Connor the whole roll.  Connor's eyes light up.**

                    CONNOR
Wow! Thanks!


**INT. ELEGANT RESTAURANT - NIGHT - ON MIKE waiting at the Maitre d's stand.  Martha enters and almost walks into him.**

                    MARTHA
Oh, it's you!

                    MIKE
Martha!  I - uh - I'm meeting someone here.

                    MARTHA
So am I.

**MAITRE D' enters, looks at Martha, and bows slightly.**

                    MAITRE D'
You are Martha Brownley?  Nice To Meet You, Madame.

                    MARTHA
Yes...  Yes, Nice To Meet You.

**Maitre D' looks at Mike and bows slightly.**

    MAITRE D'
You are Mike Brownley?  Nice To Meet You, Monsieur.

    MIKE
Yes, umm...  Nice To Meet You.

    MAITRE D'
This way, please, both of you.

**Maitre D' exits.  Martha and Mike exit following him.**


**INT. ELEGANT RESTAURANT - NIGHT - ON MAITRE D' showing Mike and Martha to a secluded table with lit candles and a lavish bouquet of flowers.  He sets two menus and a wine list on the table.**

    MARTHA
Wait, this can't be right.

    MAITRE D'
But, I assure you, it is correct.  This reservation came with very special instructions, Madame.  Please enjoy your meal.

**Maitre D' exits.**
**Mike and Martha examine the card on the bouquet.**

    MIKE
**(reading off card)**
With special compliments to the Brownley's - 'Nice To Meet You.'

    MIKE
**(to Martha)**
You joined a dating service?

**MARTHA**
Obviously, so did you!

**MIKE**
Well, then, let's have dinner Martina.

**MARTHA**
Martina?  Who's Martina?

**MIKE**
I thought she was my date.

**MARTHA**
She must be having dinner with Miguel.  He was supposed to be my date.

**Martha and Mike sit down.**

**MIKE**
How did you come up with a name like Martina?

**MARTHA**
I didn't.  It must have been the computer.

**MIKE**
Un-huh.

**MARTHA**
Besides, you wanted to date Martina, **Miguel.**

**MIKE**
Uh, that must have been the computer, too.

**MARTHA**
Un-huh.

**MIKE**
Have you tried any good wines lately?

MARTHA
**(Remembers her dates.)**
Nothing I care to order tonight.  How about you?

MIKE
**(Remembers his dates.)**
Yes, but I think I'd prefer our usual Beaujolais.

MARTHA
That's fine with me.  I'm ordering the roast beef.

MIKE
Sounds good.  I'll have that too.

**The WAITER enters.**

MIKE
We've decided.  We'll both have the roast beef - medium rare and a bottle of  Beaujolais.

WAITER
Very good, Monsieur.

**The Waiter exits.**

MIKE
Where's Connor tonight?

MARTHA
Maureen is staying with him.  He's unhappy, because he knows I have a date tonight.

MIKE
Yes, he expressed that to me, too.  I know he'll get over it eventually, but it really bothers me.  It's a hard adjustment for a kid.

#### MARTHA

I agree. You know, I didn't actually tell him I had a date, although he surmised it. All day, I've been wondering if that was the right way to handle it.

#### MIKE

I wish I knew... So, is this your first date with 'Nice To Meet You'?

#### MARTHA

No, it's my third. How about you?

#### MIKE

Fourth, if you count being stood up last night.

#### MARTHA

I don't think that counts. I guess I have to ask... Have you met anyone you liked?

#### MIKE

No, not at all. How were your dates?

#### MARTHA

Umm, I'd have to say... Well, not too bad.

#### MIKE

Mine were awful, just awful.

#### MARTHA

Actually, mine were pretty awful, too.

**They share a laugh.**
**Waiter enters and serves the wine.**
**They both taste it and nod.**
**Waiter exits.**

#### MIKE

Just as an example of how bad they were, my first date wanted to know if Turkey was near the Mediterranean.

MARTHA
**(laughing)**
That's good.  Mine wanted me to help him pick out a diamond for his girlfriend.

MIKE
Oh, that's even better.  My other date got soused, so now I know all about the daytime soap opera characters.

MARTHA
Ohh...  I bet you were intrigued with that...  Because of my other date, I can identify with football widows.

MIKE
Oh, no!  I can just see you...

MARTHA
The more I think about my dates, the more ridiculous they were. I had no fun at all.

MIKE
Same here.  They were absurd.

MARTHA
You know it's really pathetic when you have more fun with the man you're divorcing.

MIKE
I had more fun with you that time we were snowed in at the Buffalo airport than I've had on either of these dates.

MARTHA
And that wasn't exactly our finest hour was it?

MIKE
No, it wasn't.  Then again, you know, Martha, maybe it was.  We

used to really stick together through it all. I don't really know what happened to us.

### MARTHA

You turned into a vagabond, instead of a husband. Remember weeks away from home without hardly more than a postcard?

### MIKE

Aahh, yes. My absence coincided with your transformation into a materialistic hard-bitten sales person.

### MARTHA

Here we go again! This is where I remind you about how important it is to make some money, instead of devoting your whole life to academics.

### MIKE

That's right, suddenly all you cared about was the money. You always have to rub it in don't you? Just as my career was about to break, you decided yours was more important.

### MARTHA

Maybe this was a bad idea. There's nothing new to say here, and I really don't want to fight this fight all over again.

### MIKE

You're right about not wanting to fight, but I do realize I was wrong about some things.

### MARTHA

Such as...

### MIKE

For example, the traveling. One of my dates wanted to travel with me. She claimed she'd die of loneliness without me at her side.

MARTHA
**(laughs)**
Are you serious?


MIKE
Almost...  But, seriously, I was unfair to expect you to be a drudge at home.


MARTHA
I'm glad to hear you say that.  As a matter of fact, one of my dates was cheering me on in my sales endeavors when I realized that academics and time off are important to me too.


MIKE
Thank you...  Martha, I do miss having a real home.


MARTHA
And I wish I could have a weekend off to enjoy mine.


MIKE
So, take this weekend off and spend it with me.


MARTHA
What, you're staying in town for two whole days?


MIKE
Actually, no, I'm going to give a talk up the coast.  It's a beautiful drive.  Why don't you come with me?  I only have to give a short talk.  Then I'm free for a weekend on the shore.


MARTHA
I've got to think about it. I'm not sure...  I mean, I don't know if...


MIKE
Why not?  Do you have another date planned?


MARTHA
I'll arrange it with my office. If you can be flexible, so can I.

Could you get your mother to sit with Connor?

MIKE
Yes, I'm sure I can talk her into it.

MARTHA
That sounds good.

MIKE
What about the big question?

MARTHA
You mean, what to tell Connor? Why not the truth?

MIKE
Because, I don't want to get his hopes up. I mean, nothing's definite between us, at least not yet, and I feel he's in a fragile state right now.

MARTHA
Nothing's definite, but I don't want to keep him in the dark again. It's just not fair to him. I think dishonesty would be more damaging.

MIKE
You're right. We'll tell him the truth. We're only going away for a couple of days and trying things out for a little while...

MARTHA
I'll make it clear this is just an experiment. And it is just an experiment... for now.

**INT. FOYER OF BROWNLEY HOME - DAY - ON MARTHA standing at the foot of the stairs.**

MARTHA
Connor! Could you come down here? I want to talk to you.

CONNOR (O.S.)
Alright, Mom!

**We hear CONNOR'S FOOTSTEPS.**
**Connor enters from the stairs.**

CONNOR
Yeah, Mom, what is it?

MARTHA
This weekend I'm going away, and you're staying with Grandma.

CONNOR
Where are you going?

MARTHA
Now, don't get your hopes up. This doesn't mean anything. Understand?

CONNOR
I guess.

MARTHA
Your Dad and I are going to one of his lectures this weekend. Now, remember, nothing is definite.

CONNOR
Mom! You're going with Dad? That's great!

MARTHA
Don't get excited. It's only a weekend. Understand?

CONNOR
That rocks!

MARTHA
Now get back to your homework.

**INT. CONNOR'S BEDROOM - DAY - ON CONNOR working at his computer. The TELEPHONE RINGS downstairs.**

**INSERT CLOSE SHOT of computer screen with 'Nice To Meet You' background and adjacent article entitled, 'Taking Down Your Web-Site.'**

**BACK TO SCENE There is a KNOCK ON THE DOOR and Martha enters.**

> MARTHA
> Connor, Grandma's going to pick you up.... What are you doing?

> CONNOR
> Nothing.

**Martha walks over and looks closer at the computer.**

> MARTHA
> Connor! You didn't! Did you...?

> CONNOR
> Awww... Mom...

> MARTHA
> Coincidences my foot! Connor, I can't believe you were capable of this!

> CONNOR
> I was just trying to help.

> MARTHA
> You fixed me up with Bill and Seymour?

**CONNOR**
And with Dad...

**MARTHA**
How did you pick Bill and Seymour?

**CONNOR**
Well, I had to pick people I knew, so that I'd know you wouldn't like them.

**MARTHA**
Why did you pick them so that I wouldn't like them?

**CONNOR**
So that you'd get back with Dad. I figured that if you had a rotten time on your dates, Dad would start looking better, and you'd start seeing him again.

**MARTHA**
How did you know I wouldn't like any of them?

**CONNOR**
Because, I really know them, and you don't.

**MARTHA**
Connor...

**CONNOR**
Mom, you didn't like them!

**MARTHA**
Oh, Connor... How could you do such a terrible thing?

**CONNOR**
Was it really that bad?

## MARTHA

Yes, it was. How can you even ask that? It's wrong to manipulate people.

## CONNOR

But it worked out! I just knew you and Dad would start getting along again if you made some time for each other. This was the only way I could get you to do it.

## MARTHA

So you tricked us into it. Connor, do you understand why it was wrong?

## CONNOR

Yes, Mom.

## MARTHA

Do you promise not to do it again?

## CONNOR

Un-huh.

## MARTHA

Under the circumstances, I'll overlook it, but if it ever happens again, I'll ground you for the rest of your life. Understand?

## CONNOR

Yes, Mom, I understand.

## MARTHA

Now it's time for bed, so put the computer away and get to it.

**Martha starts to leave, then turns around.**

## MARTHA

By the way, Connor, you'd better not tell your father about this. He'd... Umm... He'd really get upset.

CONNOR
Okay, Mom, good night!

MARTHA
Good night.


**INT. MIKE'S APARTMENT - DAY - ON MIKE in his apartment looking at his mail. He opens a bill and glances at it. Then he does a double take and picks up the phone.**


**INT. KITCHEN OF BROWNLEY HOME - DAY - ON MARTHA in the kitchen. There is a KNOCK on the door and Mike enters.**

MIKE
Hi Martha, I'm here!

MARTHA
I'm almost ready.

MIKE
Okay, take your time. I'm going upstairs to see Connor!

MARTHA
Good, send Bernie downstairs. His parents just called. They'll be over to pick him up in a minute.


**INT. CONNOR'S BEDROOM - DAY - ON CONNOR AND BERNIE sitting on Connor's bed playing cards. Perky is with them. There is a KNOCK on the door. Mike enters.**

CONNOR
Dad!

**They hug each other.**

### MIKE

Hi, Connor. It's good to see you. Bernie, you'd better go downstairs, your parents are almost here.

### BERNIE

My parents? Both of them?

**Bernie exits.**

### CONNOR

I missed you Dad.

### MIKE

I missed you too, but I have to talk to you about something.

### CONNOR

About you and Mom going away? Mom already talked to me. I'm really happy you're at least getting along again.

### MIKE

I'm pleased about that too, but what I wanted to talk to you about is my credit card bill.

### CONNOR

Wh-what about it?

### MIKE

I had this charge from a florist. I didn't order any flowers, so I called to inquire about it. They received a computer order for a delivery to Chez Louis. I doubt your mother ordered them. Now what do you have to say for yourself?

### CONNOR

I think Mom really liked the flowers.

**Mike stares him down.**

**CONNOR**

Aaww, Dad... I had to. When I knew I could do this, I just had to try.

**MIKE**

Why Connor? What were you thinking of?

**CONNOR**

I wanted you and Mom to make time for each other and be together again, just like you used to be.

**MIKE**

So you started a dating service just for us? What made you think that would work?

**CONNOR**

You did. You and Mom were talking about seeing other people. I thought if you started all over again, you might start getting along with each other.

**MIKE**

And it did work, didn't it? How did you pick out dates for me?

**CONNOR**

Well, I went by who I disliked. I figured if you ever actually talked to them, you wouldn't like them either. I didn't want to pick anyone you might like, except for Mom, of course.

**MIKE**

That wasn't fair to them. You know that don't you?

**CONNOR**

Uh, I didn't think about that.

**MIKE**

Connor, I don't want you to think I approve, but I guess I understand. We'll still talk more about it next week.

**CONNOR**
Okay, Dad.

**MIKE**
All things considered, I think it's best if we don't tell your mother about this, all right?

**CONNOR**
All right, Dad.

**Mike exits. Connor runs over and hugs Perky.**

**CONNOR**
Perky! We did it! We did it!

**Bernie enters.**

**BERNIE**
I gotta get my stuff and go. My mother called my dad and they figured out how long I've been gone.

**CONNOR**
Bernie, my dad figured out it was me. They're sort of back together, and I'm not even really in trouble yet.

**BERNIE**
That's great! How'd you do it?

**CONNOR**
You were right. It worked out, so they couldn't get too mad. Then they'd have to tell each other.

**BERNIE**
Look, I'll call you later. My parents are here, both of them, together... Are they ever steamed!

**CONNOR**
That's great too!

BERNIE
Yeah, I guess it is.

**They punch each other as Bernie exits.**

**FADE OUT.**

## THE END

## About the Author

Katherine Traphagen has written two novels, **Anomaly Adventures** and **Skeletal Scramble**, as well as a screenplay, **Nice To Meet You.**

Originally from Erie, Pennsylvania, she lived in Boston, Massachusetts for fifteen years. She graduated from Michigan State University in 1982.

Ms. Traphagen's main career has been Blood Banking. She has also forayed into genealogy, real estate, and tarot card reading.